BOOKS BY JOHN L. LOVE

Unspoken Reality

Love

The Power Within

Street Style

The 7 Keys Of Success

Flawless Potential

Pets Everyday Training Solutions

The Evolution Of Discrimination

Forced By Any Means Necessary

Gang Eighty-Fith

Seven Times The Deadly Sinner

Business Is Business, No Skin Color Required

BUSINESS IS BUSINESS, NO **SKIN COLOR** REQUIRED

By John L. Love

BUSINESS IS BUSINESS, NO SKIN COLOR REQUIRED

CONTENTS

BUSINESS IS BUSINESS,

NO **SKIN COLOR**

REQUIRED

A step by step guide to becoming a successful business owner, regardless of skin color or ethnic background.

By John L. Love

BUSINESS **IS JUST** BUSINESS!

When it comes to "**Supporting Black Businesses**" I personally stand for ALL BUSINESSES! This message is stated towards the massive "Unnecessary" "support black businesses" debate. My thought is this, anyone will support anyone, it's personally up to us (Entrepreneurs) to create or re-create things that people want or need. Not arguing or going into an ALL OUT **RACE WAR**. I myself am a "**BLACK AMERICAN MAN**" & I simply support any potential business that serves a purpose for everyday needs. I don't care who the owner is, all I focus on is "What they are selling me" & "How convenient is the location to residential areas" in addition to this note, if the store or businesses are selling what people want, then people will shop there or condone their business there, all any race/ ethnic background have to do is open up businesses that draws in customers or sell items people actually want or need; then watch the money fly until then…..Business will always be Business….STOP MAKING it PERSONAL!

John Lee Love
Minneapolis, Minnesota
January 2016

BUSINESS NOTES

COMPARE
OTHER "RACES"
IN BUSINESS

Now when it comes to the "TOP SUCCESSFUL" "Races" in business, a lot of different ethnics think of "one" particular "race;" & that's" Caucasians"

But why?

Another is the Arabians', along with Africans (from Africa), & there is Indians (from India), & lastly, Somalien's, & Latino's.

Now, one can only wonder; how can all of them, except (Caucasians) who come to America, & not only build, but OWN multiple BUSINESSES!

What is their secret?

Their secret is NO SECRET, all they are doing, is supporting their selves/ investing in their selves. Along with NOT investing in the simple minded things a lot of us Americans invest in, like "shoes & clothes," also, the other thing they are doing...which is the main thing, & that's NOT KILLING EACH OTHER!

They work together, & help each other succeed in the process, stepping on one another's "Toes" isn't in their category....hint, hint, hint.

There are plenty other amazing things that are incredibly simple when it comes to business. Throughout this book, I'll explain the simple step by step process you'll need to understand, before you go for the head dive in business. I will also include "writing space" for you to freely take "Business" notes for your own personal gain & memorization towards your step ladder to success! On the following pages will also give you the opportunity to do practice exercises along with notes as you build your business.

In is section I want you to (get to know) your competition! Yes they are your personal competition. This exercise will not only help you get well prepared, but in addition; extremely familiar with what you WILL BE UP AGAINST!
In other words, KNOW the BATTLE before the FIGHT!

TALK TO "3" DIFFERENT "RACES" IN BUSINESS

RACE ETHNIC_____

BUSINESS TYPE_____

_____

YEARS IN BUSINESS_____

TIME TOOK TO BUILD COMPANY_____

LOCATION FOR REVENUE_____

MONEY INVESTED $_____

BUILDING COST/ IF ANY $_____

SCHOOL DEGREE/ OR SEMINAR_____

BUSINESS LOAN AMOUNT/IF ANY $_____

RACE ETHNIC_____

BUSINESS TYPE_____

_____

YEARS IN BUSINESS_____

TIME TOOK TO BUILD COMPANY_____

LOCATION FOR REVENUE_____

MONEY INVESTED $_____

BUILDING COST/ IF ANY $_____

SCHOOL DEGREE/ OR SEMINAR_____

BUSINESS LOAN AMOUNT/IF ANY $_____

RACE ETHNIC_____

BUSINESS TYPE_____

_____

YEARS IN BUSINESS_____

TIME TOOK TO BUILD COMPANY_____

LOCATION FOR REVENUE_____

MONEY INVESTED $_____

BUILDING COST/ IF ANY $_____

SCHOOL DEGREE/ OR SEMINAR_____

BUSINESS LOAN AMOUNT/IF ANY $_____

BELIEVE YOU
CAN BE
SUCCESSFUL

Determination is one of the main keys, in ANY THING YOU CHOOSE TO DO!
This is a known TRUE FACT!
Without it, you'll fail miserably.
So just take the time to build yourself up; so you'll be ready for the tough competitors coming your way. First, know ALL of your abilities as a business individual, next, know ALL of your strengths, as well as your weaknesses!

This can go either way, in your favor, along with your opponents favor.
Always remember: "Your strengths" is your opponents' weaknesses, & "Your weaknesses" is your opponents' strengths. In other words, what you CAN'T do, someone else CAN do! & vice-versa. No one person is good at everything; & never assume you're in a winning one-sided battle....those are highly rare in many cases, & your opponent may or may not have already figured them out before you did, so stay sharp!

In the following pages, I want you to get to know your (Business) self/ mind frame. In addition to this, I want you to understand "3" of your main STRENGTHS as well as WEAKNESSES! So equaling a TOTAL of "6" this is a small, but BIG KEY to understand during the business process of your journey.

The following page's allows you to complete this exercise, BEFORE you go into business!

STRENGTH
#1_____

_____

_____

STRENGTH
#2_____

_____

_____

STRENGTH
#3_____

_____

_____

WEAKNESS
#1_____

_____

_____

WEAKNESS
#2_____

_____

_____

WEAKNESS
#3_____

_____

_____

LOSE
UNNECESSARY
THINGS/ PEOPLE

Now, when I say "lose things" I mean to change things about yourself, like: bad habits, bad people, drugs, alcohol, ect. You get the picture.

So for starters, your mind frame should be the first thing in ORDER!

How to do that is labeled in the (previous) exercise, but I'll still give extra pointers here for a more in-depth understanding.

Now what worked for me, was my old friends, you know...the ones who don't call you all the time; I like to call them "extra" unnecessary friends. Or "extra" baggage.

In addition to losing people, try getting rid of personal things that YOU DO, that annoy people, & you know what YOU DO!

With that being said, get rid of it the best you can, I say this because this is a HORIBLE factor that can, & WILL damage your potential future business or business partners. Also, within the same time frame, (while losing) all of your bad habits, study ALL of your GOOD habits. This will help you stay sharp on what you do need, & to stay even sharper on what you don't need in your life from here on out.

In this next exercise I want you to take the time to REALLY THINK....I MEAN REALLY THINK of ALL of your BAD habits, including bad people, & get RID of them ALL!!!

So on the next following pages I will allow writing space for at least "6" of each "4" different categories, 6 bad people, 6 bad habits, 6 positive things to upgrade, & getting to know 6 positive people to know work on from here on out. Like the saying goes "out with the old, & in with the new."

BAD PERSON #1_____

BAD PERSON #2_____

BAD PERSON #3_____

BAD PERSON #4_____

BAD PERSON #5_____

BAD PERSON #6_____

BAD HABITS #1_____

BAD HABITS #2_____

BAD HABITS #3_____

BAD HABITS #4_____

BAD HABITS #5_____

BAD HABITS #6_____

POSITIVE THING #1_____

POSITIVE THING #2_____

POSITIVE THING #3_____

POSITIVE THING #4_____

POSITIVE THING #5_____

POSITIVE THING #6_____

POSITIVE PERSON #1_____

POSITIVE PERSON #2_____

POSITIVE PERSON #3_____

POSITIVE PERSON #4_____

POSITIVE PERSON #5_____

POSITIVE PERSON #6_____

BUILD A
POSITIVE IMAGE

You may have heard the phrase, "Birds with feathers, flock together"
If not, then you'll need to learn it now. It basically means, if you "Hangout" with people that do CERTAIN things, chances are, you DO those same things. So if your friends do drugs, then chances are, you do them too; or why else would you "hangout" with people who use drugs' right?
So treat your upcoming business the same. Apply these same principles to obtaining a new business image for yourself.
Now a business "image" can be a couple of things all wrapped in one.

The first one being your personal style.
If you are used to dressing "street" or "hood" like myself, then switching up your style....a little bit wouldn't hurt your NEW business; especially if you plan on being in a "Professional" work setting.
Always remember: "a little change NEVER HURTS anyone"
This is always true on many different levels of business.
The other parts of change have to do with your way of thinking.
Now if you are a "logical" thinker then things could be better, but if you are a "simple minded" thinking, then defiantly start the mind changing process, because when it comes to operating any business, your mind has to be expanded beyond possibilities!

In this next exercise, you'll have the opportunity to recreate your image (make it positive).
This exercise corresponds with the previous exercise, that's the main way to physically understand this portion of training. The following pages will allow you to keep track of your "body, mind, & spirit" exercise training.

BODY

FOODS TO EAT_____

WHAT NOT TO EAT_____

_____

_____

POUNDS TO LOSE_____

SMOKING HABITS / IF ANY_____

DRINKING HABITS / IF ANY_____

DRUG HABITS / IF ANY_____

EXERCISING / IF NEEDED_____

MIND

MEDITATION EXERCISE_____

VOCABULARY / DICTIONARY DEFINITIONS_____

_____

_____

_____

SLEEPING EXERCISE_____

BREATHING EXERCISE_____

SPIRIT

REMOVING BAD SPIRITS / PEOPLE_____

_____

_____

_____

ADDING GOOD PEOPLE_____

_____

_____

_____

MAKE THE
"RIGHT" FRIENDS

Friendships, they come, they go; but in the end....how much do they REALLY matter to you?

In the "Business World" friendship don't really exist, in fact, it's all about rivalry, & competition. Everyone will be trying to "one-up" each other just to be at the top!

Nobody wants to play fair anymore. So I ask you? Who can you really call your friends?

Better yet, if you were to go into business RIGHT NOW, who would you take with you?

Well to answer your question, NOBODY!

Because if you really "BOIL" it down....TRUST is the KEY that is missing in this scenario. As for friends, they will always come & go. Now is the time to be focusing on the FRIENDS you NEED. & they are the people, that sit in HIGH places.

Have you ever heard of the saying "It's not ALWAYS what you know, but WHO you know is what gets your "feet in the door" of business that is....

In this next exercise, I would like you to REALLY GET to know YOUR FRIENDS!

Find out who is business "Savvy" & who is still in "Kid mode" doing this will not only prove to you, who to work with(if you want a partner in business), & who to leave behind.

Depending on your friend (Count) this next exercise could take some time, or it can go really quickly if you have no friends at all. But in any case you can still do this exercise with family, or even (Potential) friends of interest? The following pages will allow your TOP FIVE FRIENDS! I say five because that is usually the (REAL FRIENDS) number, either that, or less! This means these are your CLOSEST FAMILY, OR FRIENDS of interest.

FRIEND/ FAMILY MEMBER NAME_____

_____

STRENGTHS IN BUSINESS_____

_____

_____

WEAKNESS IN BUSINESS_____

_____

_____

TRUSTWORTHY WITH FINANCES_____

PEOPLE PERSON / ATTITUDE ISSUES_____

EDUCATIONAL BACKGROUND_____

_____

CRIMINAL BACKGROUND_____

FRIEND/ FAMILY MEMBER NAME_____

_____

STRENGTHS IN BUSINESS_____

_____

_____

WEAKNESS IN BUSINESS_____

_____

_____

TRUSTWORTHY WITH FINANCES_____

PEOPLE PERSON / ATTITUDE ISSUES_____

EDUCATIONAL BACKGROUND_____

_____

CRIMINAL BACKGROUND_____

FRIEND/ FAMILY MEMBER NAME_____

_____

STRENGTHS IN BUSINESS_____

_____

_____

WEAKNESS IN BUSINESS_____

_____

_____

TRUSTWORTHY WITH FINANCES_____

PEOPLE PERSON / ATTITUDE ISSUES_____

EDUCATIONAL BACKGROUND_____

_____

CRIMINAL BACKGROUND_____

FRIEND/ FAMILY MEMBER NAME_____

_____

STRENGTHS IN BUSINESS_____

_____

_____

WEAKNESS IN BUSINESS_____

_____

_____

TRUSTWORTHY WITH FINANCES_____

PEOPLE PERSON / ATTITUDE ISSUES_____

EDUCATIONAL BACKGROUND_____

_____

CRIMINAL BACKGROUND_____

FRIEND/ FAMILY MEMBER NAME_____

_____

STRENGTHS IN BUSINESS_____

_____

_____

WEAKNESS IN BUSINESS_____

_____

_____

TRUSTWORTHY WITH FINANCES_____

PEOPLE PERSON / ATTITUDE ISSUES_____

EDUCATIONAL BACKGROUND_____

_____

CRIMINAL BACKGROUND_____

STOP "RECKLESS" SPENDING

Spending, spending, spending!

This is always a REAL problem in reality; this is the main KEY that can make or break ANY business!

But before we get to the main point of this.....let's take a step back to the beginning, (here & now) beginning.

Right this minute your finances might be in the ok/ tolerate category...if I'm correct?

But if I am, then let's work towards fixing it!

First let's make a chart of your NEEDS, verse your WANTS when it comes to spending money. Now since you're thinking of starting or joining a business, you got to make sure you FULLY understand finances as well as budgets. These are your two worst enemies in life....not just business.

Luckily for you I'll help you get these under control; by getting yourself under control....yep because these aren't the real problem...it's the person that's doing the spending which is the problem. So let's start making a few cut backs on eating out, extra clothe & shoe shopping, expensive restaurant foods, & so on...these are just a some of the THINGS you DON'T need to buy all the time. The next step to this process is learning to SAVE money, which can be very EASY! If I say so myself.

What I ALWAYS found to be a simple starting way to saving money, is to disguise the money like in a piggy bank. I always figured "Money I can't see, means I can't touch" also piggy bank money is the best disguise because it looks like "coins" & no big dollar bills. So chances are you'll look at it & figure "it's not enough to go shopping with" & end up walking away. But the normal way/ serious way to cut back on spending is only spending money on necessity things, like your rent, & food for your refrigerator, & other things of that nature to better help you, I have created a list of "necessity" things you NEED, versus what you may want, or can go without.

FINANCE TOTAL $_____

FINANCIAL WANTS_____

_____

_____

_____

_____

FINANCIAL NEEDS_____

_____

_____

_____

SAVINGS ACCOUNT TOTAL $_____

CHECKING ACCOUNT TOTAL $_____

PIGGY BANK / OR COIN HOLDER $_____

TOTAL SAVED MONEY $_____

BUILD
YOUR
CREDIT

If you've never had a credit card or a loan, your credit history is most likely a blank slate your credit history, as documented on your credit report, is a record of how responsibility you've repaid money you've borrowed.

Creditors & lenders use your credit history to make decisions about whether to give you a credit card or extend a loan. However, if you have no credit history, there's no record of how you might mange dept. as a result, many creditors & lenders won't lend you money. But in general, it is always a great idea to have great credit, especially if you're looking to get a "loan" from the bank!

It may seem like an impossible loop, but there are ways to build credit when you have no credit. Here's how in SIX EASY STEPS.

First. "Get a secured credit card."
A secured credit card is just like a "regular," or unsecured credit card, only you are required to put down a security deposit – typically your average $300 to $500 – to provide assurance to the creditor that you will repay your debt. Your credit limit is often the amount of your security deposit, or a percentage thereof.

Many people confuse a secured credit card with a debit card, however the two are very different. First, banks do not report card usage to the credit bureaus, as a debit card is not an extension of credit. A debit card is merely a convenient way to access the funds in your bank account.

Creditors, on the other hand, do typically report secured credit card activity to the credit bureaus, as a secured credit card is an extension of credit. Your purchases are not deducted from security deposit.

Rather, each time you charge something, you are effectively borrowing money from the credit card company & are obligated to repay that debt. As a result, how responsibility you use a secured card will affect your credit score – both positively & negatively.

Second. "Only charge what you can afford to pay off in full."
Building credit means consistently demonstrating your ability to pay back any money you borrow. Your goal is to prove creditors & lenders that you can responsibly manage debt. That's why it's smart to start small – only charge purchases that you can afford to pay off in full every month.
Unfortunately, it's not enough to open a credit card – secured or otherwise - & sit on it. If you don't use credit, you're not demonstrating anything use your card at least once a month for small purchases like inexpensive meals, gasoline & drug store essentials. Try to not charge more than 50 percent of your credit limit in a given month however, as that can take a toll on your credit score.

Third. "Pay on time every month"
The most important thing you can do to build & maintain a good credit score is paying all of your bills & Debt obligations on time every month. Even one late payment can significantly damage your credit score, especially early on.

Fourth. "Avoid applying for numerous accounts"
Each time you apply for a credit card or loan, credit score takes a small hit. & there' no point to chipping away at a credit score you're trying to build up, especially when you haven't yet demonstrated that you can handle just one credit card. Instead, use that energy to prove to yourself that you can keep the balance low on one credit card & pay the bill on time every month.

Fifth. "Check your progress by checking your credit report & score.
After six months of timely credit card payments, check your status by viewing your credit report & score.

Pay special attention to what is on your credit report & any positive or negative factors listed, so you have a better idea of what you need to work on next. Also make sure to take a look at your credit score – it will you make sense of your credit report & give you an idea of how well you're doing.

Sixth. "After a year, apply for an unsecured credit card.
Twelve months of timely payments should be enough to show your credit card company that you can responsibly manage debt. Now's the time to give your creditor a call to see if you can make the switch from credit card to an unsecured credit card. An unsecured card frees you from your security deposit obligation, will likely carry a higher credit limit & may offer useful perks like reward points.

The key to building credit is patience. Remember that having a good credit score is like having the world's best coupon book for all the biggest financial transactions in your life. It may take time to establish good credit, but once you do, you'll reap the benefits of big savings.
So once again, here is a quick recap of the six build your credit steps.

First. "Get a secured credit card"

Second. "Only charge what you can afford to pay off in full"

Third. "Pay on time every month"

Fourth. "Avoid applying for numerous accounts"

Fifth. "Check your progress by checking your credit report & score"

Sixth. "After a year, apply for an unsecured credit card"

STUDY THE
"TRADE" MARKET

5 great ways on learning how to invest into a business.

Now for you, the new investor, this is a great "stepping stone" for learning when to "Buy & Sell" a business. Since you are probably new, I would start with "stocks & bonds" now these cost different amounts of money to invest in, the higher priced versus the lower priced, can vary depending on the type of business you're investing.

So as a new investor, this will help you take your first step towards learning the basics of stock trading. One great advantage of stock trading lies in the fact that the game itself lasts a LIFETIME.

So in other words, there is always room to improve your "Buying & Selling skills in the "Business" world today.

So the first question is, "How do I get started?"

First. Open a stock broker account, find a good online stock broker & open an account. Become familiarized with the layout & take advantage of the FREE trading tools & research offered to clients only. Some brokers offer "Virtual Trading" which is beneficial because you can trade with "Play" money. A great tool for comparing online brokers can be found at stockbrokers.com

Second. Read books, books provide a wealth of information....hint...hint..hint? (like this one),
& are inexpensive compared to the cost of classes, seminars, & educational DVDs sold across the web. My personal favorite stock book is "How to make money in stocks by William O'Neal, founder of Canslim trading."

Third. Read articles, articles are a fantastic resource for education.

Try checking out "Google.com" search engine, including investopedia.com.

Fourth. Find a mentor, a mentor could be a family member, a friend, or a past or current professor, or any individual that has a fundamental understanding of the stock market. A GOOD mentor is willing to answer questions, provide help, recommend useful resources, & keep spirits up when the market gets tough. ALL successful investors of the past & present have had mentors during their early days.

Forums can be another source for question & answer. Two recommendations include "Elite Trader" & "Trade2Win." Just be careful of who you listen to. The vast majority of participants are not professional traders, let alone profitable traders. HEED ADVICE from forums with a heavy dose of salt & do not, under any circumstance, follow trade recommendations.

Fifth. Study the greats, learning about the greatest investors of years past will provide perspective, inspiration, & appreciation for the game which is the stock market. Greats include "Warren Buffett," "Jesse Livermore," & "John Templeton" & many others.

Lastly, buying your first stock!

Practicing this trading is highly effective learning for business. Practice trading in a "simulator" should be your first way of practicing!

Never start off for real, only start off in a "Testing" way therefore you DON'T lose REAL money!

With your online broker account setup, the best way to get started is to simply take the plunge & make your first trade. Start SMALL, even 1, 10, or 20 shares will serve its purpose of getting you in the game. So have fun with it, you'll need all these skills later when, or if you choose to sell or buy any business.

GET "FREE"
SCHOOL TRAINING

When it comes to starting your own business, the KEY is help. We ALL needed it, or in this case, need it. This is why I'm here to help with that need.

I know how brutal the business would can be (FROM BEFORE HAND), because I run my own business. So that is why I took the liberty in making this list of FREE online business classes & training Resources.

The following is a collection of resources offering free online business courses, seminars, & training.

'Business Startup & Growth"
My Own Business: my own business offers an extensive 16-part free online course on starting & growing a small business.

"Business Finance, & Accounting"
Bean Counting 101: a free accounting course for non-accountants.

"Simple Studies Online Accounting Lessons"
Free online lessons & tutorials for beginners.

"Financial Management Training Center"
This site offers a series of short courses, with an accompanying exam as well as several informative articles in various financial management topics.

"IRS Small Business Video & Audio Workshops"
Over the past few years the IRS has made an effort to educate the public about the complex & confusing abyss known as the US Tax Code.

These Video presentations & audio classes are designed to educate small business owners in particular about their tax rights & obligations.

"Personal Finance & Investment"
Money 101: CNN's money 101 course offer instruction on finance & money management basics such as budgeting, investing, tax planning, & insurance.

"Investing For Your Future"
This course from Cooperative Extension offers learners a step-by-step guide to investing.

"Investopedia University"
This site offers several online finance classes & tutorials covering the basics of investing, trading, retirement planning & economics.

"Free MBA Courses"
Free Management Library eMBA Courses: this free management & development program is available for for-profit businesses & nonprofits. Get an MBA education without going to college.

"London School of Business & Finance Global MBA"
This innovative program offered by the London School of Business' has the ambitious goal providing"...a first-class MBA experience that allows students all over the world to study in their own time & at their own pace." The entire accredited MBA course is available online for free. Learners can sign in via Facebook. Those who want certification can pay retroactively at the end.

"General Business Management- Various Topics"
Small Business Association (SBA): the SBA provides a helpful assortment of articles, tools, & programs to help the small business owner start & run a successful business.

"Aboutcom Small Business"
Numerous articles providing helpful tips, resources, & information on starting, running, growing, buying, & selling a small business. Also check out AboutU, which offers several free online business courses.

"SmallBizU"
This site offers several great classes on money, management, & marketing.

"MIT Sloan School of Management"
Take advantage of free online courses in various business-related topics.

"Kutztown University Online Learning Programs"
Choose from a variety of free online courses in several topics ranging from accounting, business management, legal issues, & international business. There are also courses offered in Spanish.

"SCORE Online Workshops"
The non-profit organization, SCORE offers several free workshops & webinars on its site on topics such as business planning business management, & legal considerations.

"American Management Association"
This site offers several hundred articles & white papers on various topics in business management.

"Free management Library"
This site hosts a vast storehouse of online articles & resources 15 years in the making. At the time of writing resources span 650 topics & approximately 10,000 links.

"Businessballs"
A compilation of learning materials covering various topics from business management to self-development.

"Business Marketing"
The Challenge: this is a well put together, module-based training program that will show you step-by-step how to market your business online.

"Principles of Modern Marketing"
This site provides a free series of lessons in business marketing based on the book marketing: The Core, 1/e; authored by Kevin, Hartley, Berkowitz, & Rudelius.

"Free Marketing Interviews"
An impressive collection of marketing strategy audio interviews from various marketing experts.

"Marketing Resources HubSpot"
This site offers a collection of webinars, tools, & other resources on internet marketing, SEO, blogging, social media & more.

"Economics"
Learner.org Economics USA: this site delves into the fundamentals of economic theory on both macro & micro levels, as well as US economic policy. There are 14 hours of video instruction broken down into 28 sections in addition to audio recordings.

"Into Economics Open Learning initiative"
An open courseware class on basic concepts.

"Technology & Online Commerce"
HP Learning Center: HP's online learning center provides several business courses mostly focused on using technology in business.

"Managing The Digital Enterprise"
Michael Rappa, the founder of the Institute for Advanced Analytics, designed this course to address many of the issues facing companies operating in the digital age.

The course is broken down into 15 modules with topics such as, Web Analytics, Digital Markets, Trust in Cyberspace, & Data privacy.

"Miscellaneous Business Training & Online Learning Resources"
The OpenCourseWare Consortium: a global network of higher education institution & associated organizations that offers a "broad & deep body of open educational content using a shared model."
So there you have it, as completed a nice long list to "jump start" your career in running a business. What I find easy is to dig through ALL of THESE & check them all out, once you've done that, take the time to "Log" the best ones in this book that works for you. Below is some writing space where you can keep a nice short log on what seminars or classes you have visited or plan to visit.

SCHOOL NAME_____

_____
SEMINAR NAME_____

_____
THINKING OF ATTENDING_____

SCHOOL NAME_____

_____
SEMINAR NAME_____

_____
THINKING OF ATTENDING_____

TALK TO OTHER BUSINESS OWNERS

Word of mouth can be "Keen" in today's business world. Asking around & doing your research will always help you stay one step ahead of the heard. In other words; it'll let you see what & how your competition stacks up against you. In addition to this, it allows you to well prepare yourself for the long run, as well as save you financial money that you may lose if you aren't well prepared.

Here is a list of things you should ALWAYS consider in checking when investigating any business for business building information.

First. Neighborhood location, always make sure "The Neighborhood" location is a great for generating revenue! Make sure there is "High" trafficking of residents in the town you are pursuing. Remember a lot of residents = a lot of customers!

Second. Knowing what to bring to the "Business Table" meaning what can you offer that other businesses may not be offering, or what can you improve? This is a personal "Innovative" skill one would always need to succeed in this field of work; Knowing what people want, while thinking or improving ways to deliver it to them is crucial & brings promising results for years to come.

As an entrepreneur, your main task is just that. Remember a first impression, maybe your ONLY & last impression! So make it count, & make it right.

The following 6 pages will allow you to do a simple thinking exercise on what YOU REALLY want to bring to the business world. In addition to this, I'll also give you writing space to observe 3 different businesses & 3 pages for your OWN business ideas.

BUSINESS NAME #1_____

BUSINESS TYPE_____

WHO THEY EMPLOYED_____

WHY THEY CHOOSE THE TYPE OF BUSINESS_____

_____

_____

WHY THEY CHOOSE THEIR LOCATION FOR BUSINESS_

_____

_____

DO THEY PARTNERSHIP WITH OTHER COMPANIES ?_

_____

BUSINESS NAME #2_____

BUSINESS TYPE_____

WHO THEY EMPLOYED_____

WHY THEY CHOOSE THE TYPE OF BUSINESS_____

_____

_____

WHY THEY CHOOSE THEIR LOCATION FOR BUSINESS_

_____

_____

DO THEY PARTNERSHIP WITH OTHER COMPANIES ?_

_____

BUSINESS NAME #3_____

BUSINESS TYPE_____

WHO THEY EMPLOYED_____

WHY THEY CHOOSE THE TYPE OF BUSINESS_____

_____

_____

WHY THEY CHOOSE THEIR LOCATION FOR BUSINESS_

_____

_____

DO THEY PARTNERSHIP WITH OTHER COMPANIES ?__

_____

BUSINESS NAME #1_____

BUSINESS TYPE_____

WHO YOU WILL HIRE_____

WHY YOU CHOOSE THIS TYPE OF BUSINESS_____

_____

_____

WHY YOU CHOOSE THIS LOCATION FOR BUSINESS_

_____

_____

WILL YOU PARTNERSHIP WITH OTHER COMPANIES ?_

_____

BUSINESS NAME #2_____

BUSINESS TYPE_____

WHO YOU WILL HIRE_____

WHY YOU CHOOSE THIS TYPE OF BUSINESS_____

_____

_____

WHY YOU CHOOSE THIS LOCATION FOR BUSINESS_

_____

_____

WILL YOU PARTNERSHIP WITH OTHER COMPANIES ?_

_____

BUSINESS NAME #3_____

BUSINESS TYPE_____

WHO YOU WILL HIRE_____

WHY YOU CHOOSE THIS TYPE OF BUSINESS_____

_____

_____

WHY YOU CHOOSE THIS LOCATION FOR BUSINESS_

_____

_____

WILL YOU PARTNERSHIP WITH OTHER COMPANIES ?_

_____

INVEST LIKE
AN ENTREPRENEUR

When it comes to building or owning a business, everyone likes to just "dive" right in.

But diving in' is never the smart way to conduct ANY type of business. I know this from beforehand due to the mistakes I made in my previous business.

My first mistake was NOT knowing how to FRANCHISE my products properly. Take it from me; advertising is a STRONG KEY to generating revenue. No one can buy what they don't know about, products need to stand out; so your potential buyers can shop with you, or do business with you.

My second mistake was REALLY my FIRST mistake, & that was putting too much on my plate....in other words, giving my store too much product for me to handle or keep track of. The only thing I had on my mind was...."I need to fill my store"

When I should have been thinking, "I'll sell only a hand full of items, & then I'll see how things go from there."

When starting any business, these are key factors that can cause bankruptcy, & loss, stolen, & even damaged product, all because you couldn't keep track of what you could handle; instead of what you couldn't.

Just be careful of how you start off, & keep a closetful eye on your product. In this exercise try checking out some major businesses to see how much product (depending on business size) is a good enough size to start off with. This comparison should ONLY correspond with YOUR business that you are working on building or have built. The following pages, will allow you to take & keep track of notes that pertain your business production (size) as well as comparing the other businesses production (size) of your choice. Do this comparison for "3" different business sizes, small, medium, & large business sizes to be exact.

(Your) Small business name_____

_____

NAMES OF PRODUCTS_____

_____

_____

_____

_____

_____

_____

QUANTITY PRODUCT #1_____

QUANTITY PRODUCT #2_____

QUANTITY PRODUCT #3_____

QUANTITY PRODUCT #4_____

QUANTITY PRODUCT #5_____

QUANTITY PRODUCT #6_____

QUANTITY PRODUCT #7_____

(your) Medium business name_____

_____

NAMES OF PRODUCTS_____

_____

_____

_____

_____

_____

_____

QUANTITY PRODUCT #1_____

QUANTITY PRODUCT #2_____

QUANTITY PRODUCT #3_____

QUANTITY PRODUCT #4_____

QUANTITY PRODUCT #5_____

QUANTITY PRODUCT #6_____

QUANTITY PRODUCT #7_____

(your) large business name_____

_____

NAMES OF PRODUCTS_____

_____

_____

_____

_____

_____

_____

QUANTITY PRODUCT #1_____

QUANTITY PRODUCT #2_____

QUANTITY PRODUCT #3_____

QUANTITY PRODUCT #4_____

QUANTITY PRODUCT #5_____

QUANTITY PRODUCT #6_____

QUANTITY PRODUCT #7_____

(their) small business name_____

_____

NAMES OF PRODUCTS_____

_____

_____

_____

_____

_____

_____

QUANTITY PRODUCT #1_____

QUANTITY PRODUCT #2_____

QUANTITY PRODUCT #3_____

QUANTITY PRODUCT #4_____

QUANTITY PRODUCT #5_____

QUANTITY PRODUCT #6_____

QUANTITY PRODUCT #7_____

(their) medium business name_____

_____

NAMES OF PRODUCTS_____

_____

_____

_____

_____

_____

_____

QUANTITY PRODUCT #1_____

QUANTITY PRODUCT #2_____

QUANTITY PRODUCT #3_____

QUANTITY PRODUCT #4_____

QUANTITY PRODUCT #5_____

QUANTITY PRODUCT #6_____

QUANTITY PRODUCT #7_____

(their) large business name_____

_____

NAMES OF PRODUCTS_____

_____

_____

_____

_____

_____

_____

QUANTITY PRODUCT #1_____

QUANTITY PRODUCT #2_____

QUANTITY PRODUCT #3_____

QUANTITY PRODUCT #4_____

QUANTITY PRODUCT #5_____

QUANTITY PRODUCT #6_____

QUANTITY PRODUCT #7_____

INVEST IN
OTHER BUSINESSES

The most important question for a business investor is where to focus attention. What makes one company more interesting than another? There are 28 million businesses or more in the U.S., but few research services. This provides great opportunities for above-market returns but also means investors must have an approach for determining which companies are worth focusing on. After many years of investing in private companies, in the next few pages I listed a list of things I personally look at when I see a new company. This list is not intended to be all inclusive; it's intended only to serve as a starting point. The principles behind this list could apply to many industries, but they are especially relevant to consumer & retail business. The industries in which I have the most experience.

Gross margin:
Gross margin is the percentage difference between what a product sells for in the market (revenue) & what it costs to produce that product (cost of goods sold, or COGS)> this ratio is critical because it is what allows a company to invest in all the other areas needed to get the product to market such as marketing & distributions. Gross margins can vary by industry, & even by categories within an industry, but razor-thin gross margins leave no room for error. In private equity, I focused on investing in categories that had higher gross margins & thus could sustain increased costs more easily. Examples of higher gross margin categories include personal care, premium pet food, & natural & organic products. It's very important to keep in mind that gross margin expansion is very difficult. Focusing on creating products with better margins, automating production or getting lower prices for ingredients can help, but the instances where gross margin improvement drives outsized investment returns are rare.

Brand strength:

This is often the toughest thing to assess in a small company, but an investor needs to ask them self, "Does this brand offer something unique?" most companies go wrong by providing the same brand, just different packaging with a beautiful design.

Ceo:

In any business, you are investing as much in the leadership as you are in the product or company. As a result, you need to invest behind a CEO in whom you believe. As part of your initial diligence, reference checks & third-party background checks are a most. Beyond that, there isn't a formula for evaluating leadership talent but you should do what every investor does-spend time asking questions. Get on a conference call & probe on issues you think are important.

Does this person understand their business, have a passion for the product, & have what it takes to persevere?

Exit Prospects:

Many people think that if they build a great company there will always be a home for it, but in certain industries that's not the case. If the company has visions of selling to a strategic acquirer, it should be able to 1) identify who these likely "strategics" are, 2) determine what their acquisition strategies have been, & 3) be able to explain why that business should be attractive to a strategic acquirer.

Recurring revenue:

Recurring revenue is the portion of the revenue that is going to continue in the future. It provides a nice base (ideally a growing base) of revenue on which management can rely while focusing on ways to grow the business. It's especially valuable because the cost of acquiring a new customer is typically about six times the cost of keeping an existing customer. In consumer products recurring revenue comes from repeat purchase. This only applies to your business if you are ordering multiples of the same product.

HOW TO BUY OR
SELL A BUSINESS

For some people, buying an existing business is a better option than starting one from scratch. Why? Because someone else has done much of the legwork for you, such as establishing a customer base, hiring employees, & negotiating a lease still, you'll need to do some thorough research to make sure that what you see is what you'll get.

What type of business should you buy?
Look for a business that has some connection to types of work you've done in the past, classes you've taken, or perhaps. Skills you've developed through a hobby. It's almost always a mistake to buy a business you know little about, no matter how good it looks. For one thing, your lack of knowledge about the industry might cause you to overpay. & if you do buy the business, you'll have to struggle up a steep learning curve afterward.

But do try to choose a business that you're excited by. It's easier to succeed in business when you enjoy the work you're doing.

Finding a business to buy:
As you begin your hunt for the perfect company, consider starting close to home. For instance, if you're currently employed by a small business you like, find out whether the present owner would consider selling. Or ask business associates & friends for leads on similar businesses that may be on the market. Many of the best business opportunities surface by word of mouth - & are snapped up before their owners ever list them for sale.

Other avenues to explore include newspaper or online ads, trade associations, real estate brokers, & business suppliers.

Finally, there are business brokers – people who earn a commission from business owners who need help finding buyers. It's fine to use a broker to help locate a business opportunity, but it's foolish to rely on a broker – who doesn't make a commission until a sale is made – for advice about the quality of a business or the fairness of its selling price.

Research the business's history & finances:
Before you seriously consider buying a particular business, find out as much as you can about it. Thoroughly review copies of the business's certified financial records, including cash flow statements, balance sheets, accounts payable & receivable employee files including benefits & any employee contracts, & major contracts & leases, as well as any lawsuits & other relevant information.

This review (lawyers call it "due diligence") will not only help you understand how the company ticks, but will alert you to potential problems. For instance, if a major contract like a lease prohibits you from taking it over without the landlord or other party's permission, you won't want to finalize the deal without getting that permission. Don't be shy about asking for information about the business, & if the seller refuses to supply it, or if you find any misinformation, this may be a sign that you should look elsewhere. For an extensive list of questions you'll want answered before committing to a purchase.

Closing the deal:
If you've thoroughly investigated a company & wish to go ahead with a purchase, there are a few more steps you'll have to take. First, you & the owner will have to agree on a fair purchase price. A good way to do this is to hire an experienced appraiser. Next, you & the business owner will agree on which assets you'll buy (such as a building & equipment) & the terms of payment. Most often, business are purchased on an installment plan, with a sizable down payment.

After you have outlined the terms on which you & the seller agree, you'll need to create a written sales agreement & possibly have a lawyer review it before you sign on the dotted line.

Determine a realistic price range:
If you price your business too high, you'll scare away buyers. If you price it too low, you'll lose out. To figure out a range that's realistic, you can use one of several methods - & then maybe blend the results. For example, you can base the price on the value of the business's assets, & add in a sum for the goodwill the business has developed. Or you can see how much comparable businesses in your industry & locale have recently sold for. Or you can use an industry formula (for example, a value based on the number of units sold annually or a multiple of average earnings).

Understand the Tax consequences:
Taxes can take a huge bite out of the money you receive for your business. It pays to know just how big that tax bite will be - & to try to lower it, most likely with help from a CPA or other tax expert.
Your tax bill will be influenced by two key factors: how your business is legally set up & - in the case of a corporation or LLC – whether you're selling the assets or the entity. Sales of all sole proprietorships & almost all partnerships are asset sales. So are the sales of many corporations & LLCs.

Look good for a sale:
The getting-ready process includes not only sprucing up your premises, but getting your numbers in good shape. Consider recasting your tax-return numbers for prospective buyers. This involve, for example, adding back to your profits discretionary expenses such as medical insurance for you & your family, travel entertainment, business vehicles, memberships & subscriptions, & salaries & bonuses paid to family members.
In recasting your tax numbers, you're not deceiving either the IRS or prospective buyers.

You're simply pointing out that the buyer may prefer not to spend Money on some of these items in the future.

Seek potential buyers:
If your business is well known, word that it's for sale may be enough. Or, possibly someone close to you – an employee, a friend, or a customer – could be a prospect. But more likely, you'll need to reach out to a bigger pool. This often includes putting ads in newspapers & trade publications, & on business-sale websites.
You may want to engage a business broker to reach more buyers, or to keep your plans from going too public too fast. Expect to pay a substantial commission.

Negotiate your deal:
In working out the terms of the sale, some key issues include whether you'll sell the business entity or just its assets, what assets (like a truck) you want to keep, & how the buyer will pay you (usually, a down payment plus installments).

Sign a sales agreement:
You'll need to put the deal in writing. Among other things, your agreement should list & value the assets the buyer is purchasing, list any contracts the buyer is assuming, & include protections that assure you'll get paid the full sale price. If you attempt the first draft of the sales agreement yourself, have it reviewed by a business lawyer to make sure you've covered all the bases.

Plan for the closing:
The closing is the meeting at which you transfer the business to the buyer. To reduce last-minute hassles, make a checklist of all the papers you & the buyer will need to bring – everything from the documents & money associated with the transfer to your alarm codes, keys, & customer lists.
File paperwork with the IRS:
After the sale, you & the buyer need to jointly complete IRS form 8594, asset acquisition statement & file it with your tax returns for the year of sale.

ENTREPRENEUR NOTES

_____

_____

_____

_____

_____

_____

_____

_____

_____

_____

_____

_____

_____

_____

_____

_____

_____

_____

_____

_____

_____

_____

_____

MEET THE AUTHOR

"JOHN LEE LOVE" is (author), & master inventor of "body-weaponry" who specializes in weapon mechanic body fusion, he is also Author of eleven other publications which eight of them are self-help guides for everyday life. He lives in Minneapolis Minnesota.